Meet Pete

Jennifer Campbell
Illustrated by Victoria Gibson

ISBN 978-0-692-84031-3

This book is dedicated to all farm and ranch kids who know why we raise livestock and put their heart and soul into caring for them.

Especially to my three who have never hesitated to help on the farm when needed. They are growing into amazing people who have a deep love and respect for livestock, the land and our lifestyle.

Pete was just six hours old when he and Emi Lou met for the first time.

When Pete was born his legs didn't work right, he couldn't stand up. If a calf can't stand, it can't drink milk from its Momma.

That meant Pete needed special attention.

It was love at first sight for Emi Lou.

She knew why they raised beef cattle on her family farm. She also knew that sometimes that meant helping the livestock that needed a little extra care.

Emi Lou knew she was up for the task.

For the first two days of Pete's life, Emi Lou spent hours in the barn with him.

She would warm and rub the tight muscles on Pete's legs, helping relax them. She worked tirelessly to help Pete.

When Emi Lou wasn't working with him, she made sure he had fresh straw to keep him warm and comfortable.

Finally Pete stood!

He was shaky and he sometimes stumbled because his muscles weren't quite strong enough yet. But Emi Lou was there to help steady him.

She was so excited because this meant that Pete would soon be running and jumping around with the other calves on their farm.

Pete loved his bottles!
And Emi Lou loved feeding Pete!

Every morning before school she made him a bottle of warm milk replacer. And every evening she made him another one.

Most calves nurse their momma cow, but Pete had Emi Lou, and Emi Lou loved feeding Pete.

When he saw her coming, no matter the time of day, he was sure she had a bottle for him and he would run towards her.

As the weather grew warmer, Pete grew stronger.

One day, Emi Lou and Pete sat outside the barn in the warm afternoon sun. She told Pete all about her family's farm and what a great place it was.

She told him about Spring on the farm.

There would be tractors in the fields, tilling the ground and planting the crops. Her family would be working from sun up until sun down.

Emi Lou's family raised corn and soybeans. Her family planted these crops in the early spring and cared for them all summer while they grew in the fields.

She told him that not only did her family raise beef cattle but they also raised pigs.

Emi Lou loved the baby pigs down at the barns, she would bring every one of them in the house if her Mom would let her. She had taken care of lots of them just like she was taking care of Pete.

However, she knew they belonged in the barns. She loved seeing them sleeping warm in a cute pig pile under the heat lamp close to the momma sow.

She looked up at the farmhouse where she and her family lived.

Her Dad and Mom worked side-by-side every day to take care of the animals and the crops. Her sister and brother loved the farm as much as Emi Lou.

They were all proud that theirs was a family farm. It was the farm her Dad had grown up on and she loved growing up here too.

Fall was Emi Lou’s favorite season.

There would be big combines in the fields harvesting the crops and tractors with grain carts to carry them away.

She told Pete the corn and soybeans from her family’s farm go to feed livestock, like him, but also had many other uses, including food for people, like her.

Lastly she talked about the other calves Pete's age in the lot with the Momma cows.

Emi Lou knew Pete was getting strong enough to be with them soon. He would still need her to feed him bottles, but he was almost ready to move to the big lot outside the barn with the other cattle.

She knew Pete would love running and jumping and playing with the other calves. It would be good for him.

A beef calf's job on the farm is to eat and grow.

Emi Lou knew that and she had done a great job making sure Pete could do his job. She would continue to do so until Pete was full grown and ready to sell.

Emi Lou loved growing up on a farm. She loved watching the livestock grow and the tractors in the fields. She loved watching her family work together She couldn't imagine growing up anywhere else.

Meet Emi Lou and Pete

The first time I saw Pete I knew he was special. Pete was born with contracted flexor tendons, which meant he couldn't extend his ankles so he couldn't stand or walk. I knew I had to help him!
I remember putting him in the back seat of my mom's pick-up truck and riding home with him. I loved spending time in the barn with him and helping him.
When he was finally able to walk I was so happy. I know the value in helping livestock both as a person and a farmer.

Thanks for sharing our story, Emi Lou

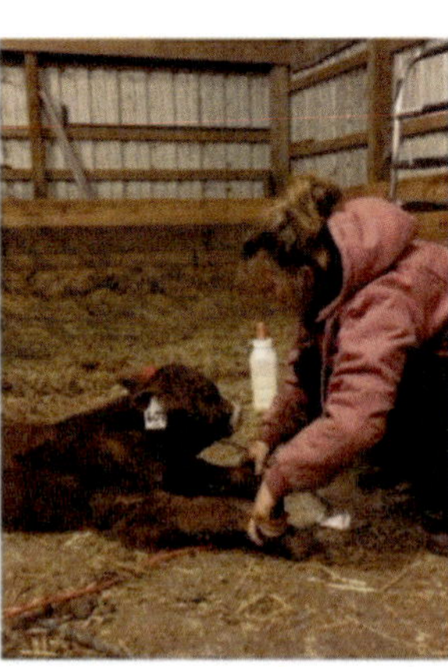

Author Jennifer Campbell lives with her husband and three kids on their row crop and livestock farm in Central Indiana. She grew up on a farm and married the farm boy just one county over. Besides working on the farm, she is passionate about spreading the story of agriculture.

Illustrator Victoria Gibson lives on a farm in central Virginia. She was a city girl that married a farm boy and quickly developed a deep love of agriculture. A mother of two girls, she enjoys painting, working with flowers, and sharing her love of all things Ag!

Made in the USA
Lexington, KY
23 June 2019